JUNIOR FIELD GUIDE

# SEA MAMMALS
## OF
# NUNAVUT

WRITTEN BY
**Jordan Hoffman**

ILLUSTRATED BY
**Kagan McLeod**

# TABLE OF CONTENTS

# WHAT IS A MAMMAL?

Mammals are a large group made up of many types of animals that share some common qualities.

Mammals have hair or fur on their bodies. Some mammals, such as whales, lose this hair shortly after they are born.

Female mammals produce milk to feed their babies. They have structures in their bodies called **mammary glands**, which make milk.

Mammal parents care for their young. Many adult mammals spend a lot of time and energy caring for their babies to help ensure they survive.

Mammals breathe using lungs and cannot breathe underwater.

There are three groups of mammals: monotremes, marsupials, and placental mammals. Mammals are divided into these groups based on how their young are born. Only placental mammals live in Nunavut.

Monotremes are mammals that lay eggs. The platypus and echidna, or spiny anteater, are the only existing monotremes.

Marsupials are mammals that carry their young in a pouch after birth. Kangaroos and koalas are examples of marsupials.

Placental mammals give birth to well-developed young. Placental mammal babies develop inside their mothers longer than other types of mammals. An organ called the placenta provides nutrients for the baby when it is growing inside its mother. Bowhead whales, walruses, wolverines, and caribou are examples of placental mammals.

**A platypus is a monotreme.**

**A kangaroo is a marsupial.**

**A bowhead whale is a placental mammal.**

# Characteristics of mammals

- Mammals are born with hair or fur.
- Mammals produce milk to feed their babies.
- Mammals care for their young.
- Mammals breathe using lungs.

## Adaptations of Sea Mammals in Nunavut

Most mammals live on land, but there are mammals that have adapted to live in the sea and in fresh water, such as lakes and rivers. Adaptations can be physical or behavioural. A physical adaptation is something on an animal's body that helps it survive in its environment. For example, muskoxen have thick fur that keeps them warm, and snowy owls have excellent vision to help them hunt lemmings. A behavioural adaptation is something an animal does that helps it survive. For example, geese fly south to spend the winter in a warmer climate.

Sea mammals are uniquely adapted for life in the sea, including their ability to swim and dive. In contrast, mammals that live on land, such as caribou, use four limbs to walk across the tundra. Other mammals, such as bats, have wings to fly. Caribou and bats can swim for short periods, but they do not have adaptations that would allow them to live in the water.

Sea mammals are adapted to life in salt water. One unique adaptation that all sea mammals have is the ability to stay underwater for long periods of time while still needing to breathe air. Sea mammals in Nunavut must also be adapted to ice, cold temperatures, different amounts of light, **predators**, and areas with different types of food.

Sea mammals in Nunavut are adapted to their environment in different ways. Some sea mammals must find ways to break through the ice to breathe or feed, while others **migrate** to areas with open water year-round. Some sea mammals spend part of their lives on land or ice, while others spend their entire lives in the water.

In this field guide, you will find out more about these animals and how they survive the extreme underwater environments in Nunavut.

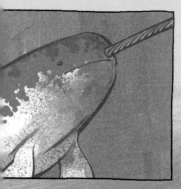

# NARWHAL

## Appearance

Narwhals are medium-sized **toothed whales**. Male narwhals weigh an average of 1800 kilograms, and females weigh an average of 1000 kilograms. Male narwhals can grow up to 5.4 metres long, and females can grow up to 5 metres long.

Adult narwhals are mostly white with dark grey heads, strips down their backs, and spots along their backs and sides. Narwhals usually get more white markings on their bodies as they age. The young of narwhals, known as calves, are completely grey when they are born.

A narwhal's tusk can be up to 3 metres long! Females also occasionally have tusks. In very rare cases, narwhals can even have two tusks that extend from their left and right front teeth.

## Range

Narwhals can be found across most of the eastern part of Nunavut, including as far north as Ellesmere Island. They are usually found as far west as Gjoa Haven on King William Island.

## Habitat

In summer, narwhals are often found in coastal areas, such as inlets with deep water that are protected from strong winds. Narwhals spend the winter in open-water areas called **polynyas**. In spring, narwhals can be found at the **floe edge** and in cracks in the ice called **leads**.

## Diet

Narwhals are **carnivores**. Narwhals feed on fish, including Greenland halibut, Arctic cod, polar cod, and Arctic char. They also eat **crustaceans**, including shrimp. They eat most of their food at the floe edge and in open-water areas during the summer.

## Reproduction

Narwhals **breed** in the spring, between March and May. Calves are born between July and August the following year after developing inside of their mothers for 14 to 15 months.

Many adult narwhals live up to about 30 years old, but they can live as long as 50 years.

## Behaviour

Groups of whales are called **pods**. You can usually find narwhals travelling in small pods of fewer than 10 whales in the summer. Sometimes narwhals gather in large pods of many hundreds of whales during their migrations in spring and fall.

Narwhals are the **prey** of orcas. When orcas are nearby, narwhals often go close to the shore in bays or inlets to stay away from them.

Scientists think male narwhals use their tusks to attract females or to battle other males. Narwhals near Pond Inlet have also been known to use their tusks to stun fish before eating them.

## Traditional Knowledge

Inuit have noticed differences between groups of narwhals based on the qualities of their tusks and body sizes. Inuit have also observed fewer narwhals in traditional areas. This might be because of increased shipping and noise levels in these areas.

# BELUGA

## Appearance

Belugas are medium-sized toothed whales. They can weigh up to 1900 kilograms. Male belugas can grow up to 4.5 metres long, and females can grow up to 3.5 metres long. Newborn belugas, known as calves, are 1.8 metres long.

Adult belugas are completely white. Beluga whale calves are born dark grey and turn lighter as they grow older.

Belugas have bulky bodies with thick skin that helps them stay warm. They have small heads with rounded foreheads. Their necks are very flexible, and they are able to move their heads in many directions.

## Found
all over
Nunavut

## Range

Belugas are found across most of Nunavut. They are found as far north as Ellesmere Island and as far south as the Belcher Islands, near Sanikiluaq. They can be found as far east as eastern Baffin Island and as far west as Kugluktuk.

## Habitat

In spring, belugas are often found along the floe edge, in ice leads, and in river **estuaries**. During the summer, belugas are found in coastal areas, usually in shallow water.

Females with calves are often found in shallow waters close to large islands or in large bays. These areas have warmer water temperatures and plenty of food. Adults without calves are often found in areas where the water depth varies and water temperatures are colder. In late summer or early fall, belugas leave river estuaries and travel to deeper waters to feed.

## Diet

Belugas are carnivores. They feed on fish, such as Arctic char, Arctic cod, Greenland halibut, and capelin. They also eat marine worms, crustaceans, and molluscs.

## Reproduction

Belugas breed between late winter and early spring. Calves are usually born in July or August after developing inside of their mothers for 13 to 14.5 months. Calves stay with their mothers to feed on their mothers' milk for two to three years.

Adult belugas can live up to 40 to 50 years old.

### Did you know?

Belugas are known to eat more than 50 different species of marine animals.

## Behaviour

Like narwhals, belugas are able to dive deep underwater. The deepest known dive of a beluga is more than 1000 metres deep!

Belugas are often found in pods of 2 to 10 whales, but it is not unusual to see larger pods.

Belugas make many different sounds, including chirps, whistles, squeaks, and clicks. If you're close to a beluga, you might be able to hear some of these sounds.

# ORCA

## Appearance

Orcas are large toothed whales. Male orcas can weigh up to 9000 kilograms, while females weigh up to 7500 kilograms. Male orcas can grow up to 10 metres long, and females can grow up to 8.5 metres long. Newborn orcas, called calves, are between 2.2 and 2.6 metres long when they are born.

Orcas are known for their black and white colours. Their bodies are black with white patches around their eyes and behind their **dorsal fins**. Their undersides are also white.

Orcas have large, distinct dorsal fins. The dorsal fins of males are straight and tall, while females have more curved dorsal fins. The dorsal fins of males are also larger than those of females.

**Found**
all over
Nunavut

## Range

Orcas are most commonly found in Hudson Bay and around Baffin Island, but they have been observed across Nunavut. There have been sightings of orcas as far west as Kugluktuk and as far north as Ellesmere Island.

## Habitat

Orcas are found in open-water areas. Orcas are not able to enter areas with ice leads or pack ice because it could cause damage to their dorsal fins. As sea ice melts in different parts of Nunavut in the summer, orcas are able to move into new areas. They are commonly found in bays and inlets while hunting for prey. Because of climate change, orcas are now being found farther north than they used to be.

## Diet

Orcas are carnivores. They are frequently known to eat narwhals and belugas, but they eat whales, walruses, and seals as well. They also eat seabirds, squid, and fish, including Greenland sharks.

## Reproduction

Orcas likely breed in the spring or early summer. Calves are likely born in the late summer or early fall after developing inside of their mothers for 16 to 17 months. Females give birth to one calf every five years.

The maximum age of orcas in the Arctic is unknown. Females can live up to 90 years, and males can live up to 60 years.

## Behaviour

Orcas migrate into Nunavut waters in late spring from **overwintering** areas between Nunavut and Greenland, near Newfoundland, or from other areas of the North Atlantic Ocean. Orcas leave Nunavut waters before freeze-up. They have occasionally been caught and trapped in sea ice as it freezes in the winter.

Orcas are often found in pods of about eight whales, but pods of up to 100 orcas have been seen. When orcas hunt large prey, like narwhals and belugas, they usually travel in larger pods.

Orcas are excellent hunters. They often work together in groups to hunt their prey. When preying on narwhals, orcas will try to push pods of narwhals into deep waters. Orcas then circle around the pods of narwhals and try to block them from reaching the surface to breathe air.

### Did you know?

Orcas are also known as killer whales because they are top predators with excellent hunting skills.

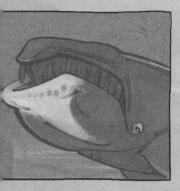

# BOWHEAD WHALE

## Appearance

Bowhead whales are large **baleen whales**. They can weigh between 75 000 and 100 000 kilograms! Male bowhead whales are 14 to 17 metres long. Females are 16 to 18 metres long, but they can grow up to 20 metres long.

Young bowhead whales, known as calves, are between 3.5 and 4.5 metres long when they are born. Calves weigh 2000 to 3000 kilograms at birth.

Unlike narwhals and belugas, bowhead whales do not have teeth. Instead, they have long, thin plates called **baleen** coming from their upper jaws. Their baleen are black with one edge that appears hairy, which they use to trap food.

Bowhead whales have thick skin and **blubber**, which helps keep them warm.

**Found**
all over
Nunavut

## Range

Bowhead whales are found across most of Nunavut. They can be found as far south as the southern Kivalliq region and southern Baffin Island, and as far north as Ellesmere Island. They are found as far east as eastern Baffin Island and as far west as Kugluktuk.

## Habitat

Bowhead whales are found in areas ranging from open water to thick pack ice with cracks. They are often found near the edge of the ice.

Bowhead whales spend the winter in areas with broken sea ice, such as northern Hudson Bay and offshore near Baffin Island. In spring, bowhead whales are found close to the floe edge. They move farther north in the summer, following the ice edge.

## Diet

Bowhead whales are carnivores, and their prey is very small. Bowhead whales feed on small shrimp-like animals called **zooplankton** that are usually found drifting near the surface of the water. They can eat up to 100 000 kilograms of zooplankton in a year. That's the equivalent of eating about 40 000 Arctic char! They also sometimes accidentally eat small fish and other small marine animals.

Bowhead whales have a unique way of eating their food. They slowly swim with their mouths open. Water with zooplankton enters their mouths, and their hair-like baleen trap zooplankton. When they close their mouths, water is forced out and the zooplankton remain in their baleen, ready to be swallowed.

## Reproduction

Bowhead whales have been known to breed throughout the year, but most breeding occurs in late winter or early spring. Females give birth to calves after 13 to 16 months, usually between April and early June.

Bowhead whales are likely the longest living mammals. Many bowhead whales likely reach between 50 and 75 years old, but some whales may live to over 200 years old!

## Behaviour

Bowhead whales are mostly found alone, except for mothers with their calves. Sometimes they may travel in small groups. In areas with lots of food, they can even be found in larger spread-out groups.

Bowhead whales can use their heads to break through ice that is over 20 centimetres thick! They can also stay underwater for up to 30 minutes in areas with sea ice. These behaviours allow bowhead whales to navigate under the ice, even though they are so large.

# WALRUS

## Appearance

Walruses are the largest members of the seal family in Canada. Adult male walruses can weigh up to 1100 kilograms, and females can weigh up to 800 kilograms. Males can grow up to 3.1 metres long, and females grow up to 2.8 metres long. Young walruses, known as calves, are about 1.25 metres long at birth.

Both male and female walruses have long ivory tusks. They can grow to almost 30 centimetres long. The female's tusks are slenderer and shorter than the male's tusks.

Walruses have large bodies covered in tough, thick skin. They have flat snouts with up to 450 whiskers that point forward from their faces. Walruses also have large front and rear flippers. Their rear flippers are triangle shaped.

## Range

Walruses are found in the eastern part of Nunavut. They are found as far south as the Belcher Islands, as far north as Ellesmere Island, and as far west as Bathurst Island.

## Habitat

Walruses are found in areas with open water and in areas with sea ice or land. In open water, they are often found at depths shallower than 100 metres where they can find clams to eat.

When walruses are not in open water, they are found on land or on the sea ice in areas called **haulouts**.

In summer and fall, when there is not as much sea ice available, walruses can be found on rocky shorelines. In winter, walruses are found on drifting sea ice with cracks or in polynyas.

## Diet

Walruses are carnivores. They mainly eat clams, which they find in large numbers. Walruses also eat seals, **invertebrates**, and seabirds.

Walruses have been known to **scavenge** dead narwhals and belugas, mainly eating their blubber and organs.

Walruses need to eat lots of clams. They can dive for up to 24 minutes and eat 40 to 60 clams during each dive. They must eat up to 25 kilograms of the soft inner parts of clams each day. Some walruses have been found with up to 6000 clams and other prey in their stomachs!

## Reproduction

Walruses breed from February to April. Breeding occurs in the water. Males fight one another for the opportunity to breed with females.

Young walruses, called calves, are born after developing inside their mothers for 11 months. Walruses give birth on land or sea ice.

Walruses can live to be up to 40 years old.

## Behaviour

Walruses found in deep water often do not eat clams but are instead known to eat seals. Inuit harvesters have observed that walruses that eat seals often have yellow tusks. These walruses are known to be more aggressive. They are also usually found by themselves or in small groups.

## Traditional Knowledge

Fermented walrus meat is called *igunaq*. Fermentation allows walrus meat to be eaten long after it is harvested. Clams found in walrus stomachs are also considered a delicacy in some Nunavut communities.

# RINGED SEAL

## Found
all over
Nunavut

## Appearance

Ringed seals are one of the smallest members of the seal family. Adult ringed seals weigh between 50 and 70 kilograms and grow to about 1.5 metres in length. Males are slightly larger than females. Young seals, known as pups, are about 60 to 65 centimetres in length and weigh between 4.5 and 5 kilograms when they are born.

Ringed seals can have either light or dark fur. Pups are born with white fur that turns silver with pale rings after they shed.

Ringed seals have round bodies. They have small heads with short snouts. Their flippers are small. They have thick claws on their front flippers.

## Range

Ringed seals can be found throughout Nunavut.

## Did you know?

Ringed seals are the most common marine mammal in the Canadian Arctic.

## Habitat

In summer, ringed seals are found in open water. They can be found in shallow or deep water as they travel in search of food. In fall, ringed seals move onto sea ice.

In winter, ringed seals are found on stable sea ice, usually over water fewer than 150 metres deep. They can be found in raised areas called pressure ridges that form on the sea ice.

## Diet

Ringed seals are carnivores. They eat many different types of prey. The fish they eat include sculpins, whitefish, Arctic cod, and capelin. They also eat very small crustaceans, including shrimp and amphipods, which are a type of zooplankton.

## Reproduction

Ringed seals breed in late spring. Breeding occurs underwater or on the sea ice.

Females carry their pups for 10 to 11 months before giving birth. Females give birth to one pup between March and May. Pups are born in dens made of snow to protect them from the environment and predators such as polar bears.

Ringed seals live for about 20 years. Some seals have been known to live up to 45 years!

## Behaviour

Ringed seals use sea ice in a unique way. They have strong claws on their front flippers that they use to dig and maintain breathing holes on the sea ice. These breathing holes can be up to 2 metres deep!

Ringed seals have many predators. They are the primary prey of polar bears. They are also the prey of orcas, Greenland sharks, and walruses.

## Traditional Knowledge

Ringed seals can be used as a source of oil for fuel, and their skin is commonly used for different types of clothing, such as *kamiit* (sealskin boots).

# HARP SEAL

## Appearance

Adult harp seals weigh between 130 and 150 kilograms and can grow to about 1.6 metres long. Males are slightly larger than females. Young harp seals, known as pups, are about 80 to 85 centimetres in length and weigh 11 kilograms when they are born.

Harp seals have grey bodies with "V"-shaped black markings on their backs and black faces. Harp seal pups are born with white coats. Pups begin to lose their white coats after 10 days and finish losing them after three weeks.

Harp seals have small heads with narrow snouts. They have short flippers. Their front flippers have thick claws, and their back flippers have smaller, narrower claws.

## Range

Harp seals are found in the eastern part of Nunavut. They are found as far south as the Belcher Islands near Sanikiluaq and as far north as Ellesmere Island. Harp seals are found as far west as Devon Island, near the community of Resolute Bay.

## Habitat

Harp seals spend their summers in the Canadian Arctic. They can be found in open water and on floating sea ice. Harp seals migrate outside of Nunavut before the sea ice forms.

## Diet

Harp seals are carnivores. Most of their diet consists of fish, such as sculpin, capelin, Greenland halibut, and Arctic cod. Harp seals also eat crustaceans, such as shrimp.

## Reproduction

Harp seals breed south of Nunavut in the spring. Breeding occurs on the sea ice. Males compete with one another to breed with females.

Females give birth to one pup each year between February and March. Pups are born on the sea ice and only stay with their mothers for about 10 to 12 days.

After 10 to 12 days, females leave their pups on their own. Pups spend another six weeks on the sea ice without eating before they enter the water to start finding their own food. During these six weeks on their own, pups can lose up to half of their body weight.

Harp seals live for 20 to 40 years.

## Behaviour

Harp seals migrate to southern Labrador, Newfoundland, and the Gulf of St. Lawrence before sea ice forms in Nunavut in the fall. After spending their winters south of Nunavut, harp seals migrate back to Nunavut in late spring. The total round-trip migration of some harp seals is up to 3000 kilometres!

Harp seals are social animals. They spend most of their lives in groups called herds. Herds can sometimes be made up of hundreds of seals. Harp seals are also sometimes found on their own.

Harp seals are not strong divers compared to other Arctic seals, such as ringed and hooded seals.

**Did you know?**

Harp seals are also called Greenland seals because they are common in Greenland.

# BEARDED SEAL

**Found all over Nunavut**

## Appearance

Bearded seals are one of the largest seals found in Nunavut. Adult bearded seals weigh between 200 and 430 kilograms and grow to between 2.1 and 2.7 metres in length. Young bearded seals, known as pups, are about 1.3 metres long and weigh about 45 kilograms when they are born.

Adult bearded seals have dark grey or brown fur on their bodies. When pups are born, they have grey or black fur with lighter fur on their heads and backs and sometimes on their back flippers.

Bearded seals have large front flippers shaped like squares with flattened ends. Their front flippers have very strong claws.

## Range

Bearded seals are found throughout Nunavut.

## Habitat

Bearded seals prefer areas with moving sea ice and areas close to open water, such as polynyas and ice leads. They are usually found in water that is fewer than 200 metres deep and close to the coast. They are sometimes found in deeper water where they can make breathing holes in the sea ice.

In summer, bearded seals can sometimes be found in estuaries and on haulouts. In winter, they can be found in polynyas.

## Diet

Bearded seals are carnivores. They mostly feed on prey found at the bottom of the ocean. Bearded seals eat fish such as sculpins and Arctic cod. They also eat squid, shrimp, crabs, clams, whelks, and marine worms.

## Reproduction

Bearded seals breed in the spring. Breeding occurs in the water. Males can compete and become aggressive with one another during the breeding season. They blow bubbles at one another and often fight.

Female bearded seals give birth to one pup each year, between March and May. Pups are born on small drifting pieces of sea ice over shallow water. Pups can enter the water a few hours after birth and quickly become good swimmers.

## Behaviour

Bearded seals are not social animals. They are usually found by themselves and occasionally in small groups. During the breeding season, males can sometimes be found together as they compete for females.

Adult male bearded seals produce many different types of sounds. In some areas they produce sounds all year, with the most sounds produced during their breeding season.

Bearded seals are not deep divers. Most dives are fewer than 10 minutes long, but bearded seals are capable of diving for 20 to 25 minutes.

# HOODED SEAL

## Appearance

Hooded seals are large seals. Male hooded seals are much larger than females. Adult male hooded seals weigh between 300 and 460 kilograms, and females weigh between 145 and 300 kilograms. Males grow to about 2.6 metres in length, and females grow to about 2.2 metres in length. Young hooded seals, known as pups, are about 1 metre long and 24 kilograms at birth.

Adult male hooded seals have a unique stretchy tissue in their noses called a hood. They can inflate their hoods to look like bright red balloons. Males also have other tissue in their noses that they inflate to form black bladders on their heads.

## Range

Hooded seals are found across eastern Baffin Island, up to the southern part of Devon Island in Lancaster Sound.

## Habitat

Hooded seals are found on drifting sea ice. They are also found in deep open water when they are feeding.

## Diet

Hooded seals are carnivores. They feed on fish such as capelin, Arctic cod, and Greenland halibut. Hooded seals also sometimes eat squid and amphipods.

## Reproduction

Hooded seals breed in late March for two to three weeks on the sea ice. Males compete with one another for females in bloody battles. Some males can breed with up to eight females during the breeding season.

Female hooded seals give birth to one pup on the sea ice in March. Pups feed on their mothers' milk for about three to five days. During this short time, pups can almost double in size from 24 to 42 kilograms.

## Did you know?

The time hooded seal pups spend feeding on their mothers' milk is the shortest time of any mammal.

## Behaviour

Like bearded seals, hooded seals are not social animals and are mostly found alone. Hooded seals are aggressive toward one another and usually do not like close contact, except for mothers and pups and during breeding. Hooded seals are sometimes found in small groups when there is a lot of food nearby and individuals are busy feeding.

Hooded seals migrate after the breeding season in late spring to early fall. They migrate on their own to feed in areas along the coast of Greenland and in Baffin Bay and Davis Strait. Hooded seals migrate back to breeding areas in late winter. Young hooded seals can sometimes be found outside of their normal ranges, as they wander when migrating.

Male hooded seals inflate their bright red hoods and black bladders to attract females during breeding season. The bladder is also a warning to other males. When females are feeding their pups, they are often surrounded by several males who compete with one another to breed with the females. These males constantly inflate their bright red hoods and black bladders to ward off other males. Males can also often fight, leading to bloody injuries.

# HARBOUR SEAL

## Appearance

Harbour seals are medium-sized seals. Male harbour seals weigh about 90 kilograms and rarely weigh above 100 kilograms. Female harbour seals weigh about 70 kilograms. Males grow to about 1.5 metres long, and females grow to about 1.4 metres long. Pups are about 80 centimetres long when they are born.

Harbour seals have fur colours that can vary from spotted brown to black to light yellow. Their fur has many different patterns of dark and light spotting.

Unlike many Arctic seals, harbour seals do not have long claws on their front flippers for digging holes through the sea ice.

## Range

Harbour seals are found in eastern Nunavut. They are usually found around eastern Baffin Island and throughout Hudson Bay to just north of Southampton Island.

## Habitat

Harbour seals are found in water along the coast, often in estuaries and rivers. They have been seen up to 200 kilometres inland as they swim up rivers! Harbour seals rely on access to open water and are found at the edge of the sea ice. They are often found in shallow water that is not deeper than 50 metres when there is sea ice.

Harbour seals haul out on land in rocky or sandy areas. They can often be found on small islands. They sometimes haul out on sea ice close to land until the ice is gone and they are able to move to land.

## Diet

Harbour seals are carnivores. Little is known about the diet of harbour seals found in the Arctic, but they likely eat fish and other types of sea animals. In Hudson Bay, harbour seals have been known to eat fish such as lake trout and lake whitefish.

## Reproduction

In Nunavut, harbour seals breed in the summer. Breeding occurs in the water. Females give birth to one pup each year in June or July. Pups are usually born on land. Pups follow their mothers into the water a few hours after birth and are able to swim and dive. Pups stay with their mothers for about one month to feed on their mothers' milk. During this month, pups can double in weight.

## Behaviour

Harbour seals often do not travel long distances. They generally stay within one area and use the same haulout sites on land. Sometimes they will migrate longer distances out of Nunavut.

Harbour seals are disturbed easily by boats, humans, and other animals. They often lie close to the water on haulouts and go into the water if they are disturbed. Some harbour seals become adapted to having regular boat traffic or human activity and do not flee into the water every time they are disturbed.

During the breeding season, male harbour seals produce sounds and dive in the water to attract females. Male harbour seals establish territories near areas where females haul out. Males also often battle with other males for access to females.

# GLOSSARY

**baleen**: a filter feeding system found in some whales, such as bowhead whales. Baleen look like bristles and are made of the same material that makes skin, hair, and fingernails.

**baleen whales**: a group of whales that have baleen plates instead of teeth in their mouths. Bowhead whales are an example of a baleen whale.

**blubber**: a dense layer of fat underneath the skin of sea mammals.

**breeding**: an activity that results in male and female animals producing babies.

**carnivore**: an animal that eats other animals as its main food.

**crustaceans**: a large group of animals that have shells on their bodies. Shrimp, crabs, lobster, krill, and copepods are examples of crustaceans.

**dorsal fin**: a fin on the back of a fish's or sea mammal's body.

**estuary**: a coastal body of water where fresh and salt water mix.

**floe edge**: an area where sea ice that is attached to land meets the open sea.

**haulout**: a place on land or ice that seals and walruses use to leave the water for a short time. Haulouts are usually used for resting or breeding.

**invertebrates**: animals without backbones. Insects and spiders are examples of invertebrates.

**lead**: a long crack in the sea ice.

**mammary glands**: the milk-producing parts of female mammals.

**migrate**: to move from one place to another according to the seasons.

**overwintering**: passing or waiting out the winter season.

**pod**: a group of whales.

**polynya**: an area of open water surrounded by sea ice.

**predator**: an animal that kills and eats other animals.

**prey**: an animal that is killed and eaten by other animals.

**scavenge**: to feed on dead animals.

**toothed whales**: a group of whales that have teeth in their mouths. Narwhals and belugas are examples of toothed whales.

**zooplankton**: very small animals that live in the water. Amphipods are an example of zooplankton.